dogfessions

secret confessions from dogs

00413981
NAUGHTY DOG
1' 10" 16

Whatever it was, I didn't do it.

COMPILED BY NIKKI MOUSTAKI

HarperCollins*Publishers*

Library of Congress catalog card number 2008922570
ISBN 978-0-06-157561-7 (trade bdg.)

Typography by Jeanne L. Hogle
1 2 3 4 5 6 7 8 9 10
❖
First Edition

This book is dedicated to Pepper and Ozzie, miniature schnauzers extraordinaire.

Acknowledgments

I would like to thank many people for making this project and book possible. First, my illustrious editors at HarperCollins, Kate Jackson and Whitney Manger—thank you for believing in this project (and thanks to Dixie, the adorable coon hound mix, for bringing your owner, Kate, to the Dogfessions.com site in the first place). Thanks also to the huge creative and marketing team at HarperCollins, who worked hard to make this book great. Thank you to my fabulous agents at the Miller Agency, Jennifer Griffin and Sharon Bowers, for believing in this project. Thank you to all the prize sponsors who graciously donated awesome pet-related products and services to the Dogfessions contest. Thank you to the Dogfessions Street Team for promoting Dogfessions wherever you go. Thanks to my friends and family for their constant support. Finally, and most importantly, I would like to offer a giant thank-you to all of the people (and their dogs) who submitted the Dogfessions that appear in this book. It couldn't have been done without your creativity and heart.

dogfessions

I have a lot of secrets about my dogs. The most shameful and perhaps the funniest is that I'm a dog trainer and I live with the naughtiest, surliest, and craziest curs in town. When I take Pepper and Ozzie, both shelter dogs, to public events, I take only one dog at a time and a purse full of treats, and I cross my fingers. Neither dog fails to astound me—the dog behaves like the finest trick-trained, well-socialized, most fun-loving mutt ever born. But back together on the streets of New York City or Miami, Florida, our hometowns, passersby keep their distance. My dogs have nipped at ankles and peed on people, they bark continuously, and they terrorize other dogs—and that's on a good day. That's my biggest Dogfession: I'm a dog trainer who owns ill-behaved dogs.

People who live with dogs understand that the relationship between human and dog is like any other: There are good days and bad days, and days when he's snoring so loud you want to knock him out of bed—no, not your husband, your pug. Dogs aren't perfect, and neither are their people. That's what makes a project like Dogfessions so wonderful. It's a place where people are free to share their most intimate secrets and feelings about their dogs—and the dogs can share back (with a little help, of course). It also doesn't hurt that dogs are fun to look at and easy to adore; they are irresistible.

Dogfessions

676A Ninth Ave., #321, New York, NY 10036

I launched Dogfessions.com in February 2007 at the various events surrounding the Westminster Kennel Club dog show and plastered Madison Square Garden with thousands of Dogfessions postcards, urging people to send in their dog secrets. I wasn't sure what would happen. Well, the Dogfessions started trickling, then pouring in. People have taken the project quite seriously. I now have a "street team" of Dogfession fans who give cards out in their own towns, leave them at pet stores and cafés, and post Dogfession links all over dog forums on the internet. Dogfessions has been called a "folk art phenomenon," and people have described it as "the next big thing for dog owners."

Whatever the case, it has become the "next big thing" for me—this project is a part of my heart and soul. I absolutely love it, nearly as much as I love dogs. When I go to my mailbox each afternoon, I'm buzzing with anticipation, hoping that there's an envelope addressed to Dogfessions in my box. I open each envelope carefully, a smile on my face, waiting to see what funny, weird, heartwarming, and sometimes heartbreaking confessions have arrived from dog lovers. I'm never disappointed. If you're holding this book in your hands, about to pore through it, you will understand. Dogfessions is an ongoing project. The next time I go to my mailbox, I hope to find *your* Dogfession there!

Sincerely,

Nikki Moustaki

Nikki Moustaki

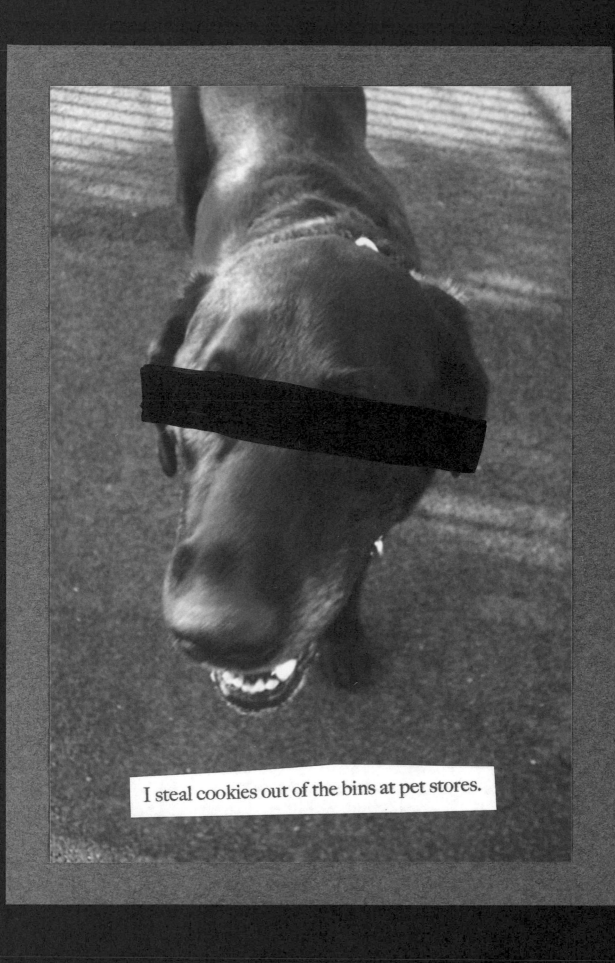

I steal cookies out of the bins at pet stores.

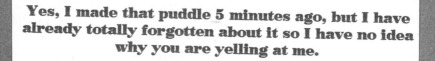

Yes, I made that puddle 5 minutes ago, but I have already totally forgotten about it so I have no idea why you are yelling at me.

Mom's taking me shopping for a sweater.

Doesn't she know I'm already wearing a fur coat?

I spent more money on the cake for my dogs birthday party (44 bucks) than I did for my husbands 50th birthday party (12 bucks).

I give my dog raspberries on his belly.

I actually paid 5 bucks a dog

Paw Readings
~Since 1697~

and had their paws read.

When people ask us what breed our dog is, we say "Beauregard Shepherd".

Often they say they have a friend with one.

They do? We made that name up.

She's a mutt!

why pay for
therapy?

a hug from
Cricket
makes me
forget all
my
problems.

Some days
I feel like
I'm being
eaten alive.

My dogs theme song is "You are my Sunshine"

I wish I'd had a digital camera for my first puppy.

when no one's watching....

i eat poo.

This photo of my friends dogs made me jealous.
My dogs don't look at me that way.

life is ruff.

I'm pretty sure that in a past life my dog was William Shakespeare.

When we watch movies with the dogs they like the chase scenes the best.

I wonder why?

sometimes . . .

. . . i eat their biscuits

When I grow up, I want to be Tyler.
She's beautiful

and she

bites.

It's
my
ONLY
Sin!

I sneak giving treats to our neighbors dog. She waits for me with one ear that perks up when she hears me coming!

After my bath I went out to
roll in the grass.
Mom thought I was
getting dry.
I was really rolling on an old,
dead frog.
Dog
Suds
What?
Smells way better to me!

I told everyone I found my dog, but really I stole him from my abusive neighbors before I moved and I'm not sorry about it. They don't deserve to have a dog – especially this wonderful dog!

Yes!

I let my dog bark
into my speech recognition
program and he kept saying
"I'd rather Nathans, I'd rather Nathans."
Does he want hotdogs?????

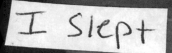

I slept

on the FLOOR

With my new puppy

for 2 ½ months!

We have our own neighborhood watch group.

EIGHT HOURS
WAITING BY THE DOOR
IS WORTH IT BECAUSE
THIS IS HOW HAPPY I GET

WHEN YOU COME HOME.

KAIA

I know labs are supposed to be water-loving, meat eating, pee-on-trees kinda dogs.

But I am a

who is afraid

NO SWIM

vegetarian

of water

and I pee like a girl.

DON'T LET THIS ANGELIC FACE FOOL YOU INSIDE, I'M ALL ROTTWEILER

Sometimes I feel guilty I br

ought Maddie to Minnesota.

Lulu

She destroyed her custom
made dog-house in less
than one hour.

It was a handmade gift.
They think we still have it.

WORK OF MEMORY ART IN PROGRESS...

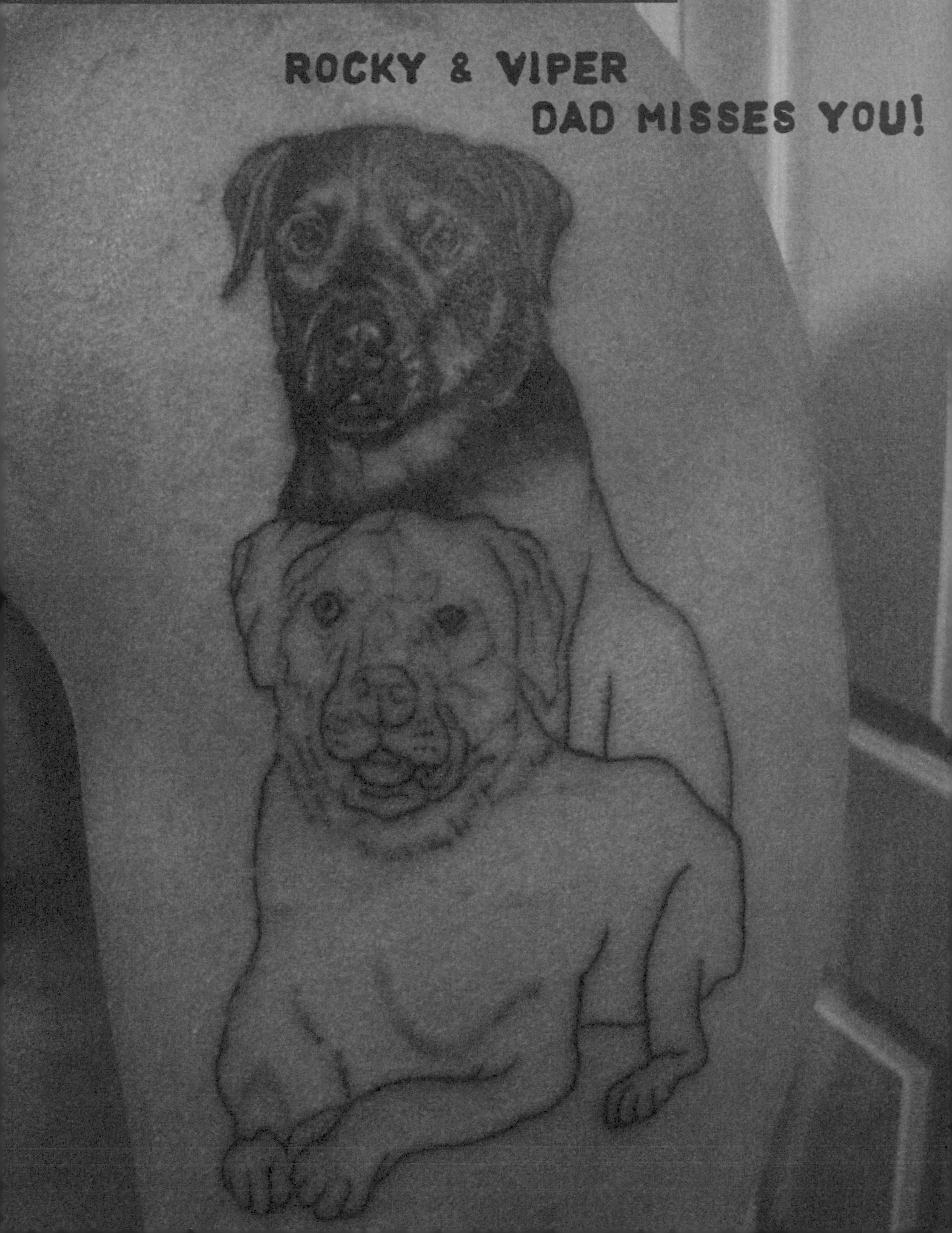

DOGFESSIONS

2

1

002BPK9

I want to be
the
Dogfessions
Mascot

We skipped another dog club meeting because we had "something important" to do.

I think enjoying the sunset with your dog is VERY important.

I think I kiss the dogs

more than I kiss my husband

IT'S TRUE
I taught Beckham everything he knows.

There is nothing finer than a nap on the porch in the summertime....

Dogfessions
676A Ninth Ave., #321, New York, NY 10036

www.dog...com

USA 24

If my dog had thumbs, I'm convinced that he would try to take over the WORLD!

→ His!

I make them sit this way for 5 minutes to let their conditioner set in.... but really it's so the other people at the dogwash can see how behaved they are.

In my past life I was a tennis pro.

It will take me a lifetime to read all these books!

I HAVE A CRUSH...ON A CAT!

THE TEXAS CATS LOVE ME FOR MY PEARLY UNDER BITE,

I AM ADORABLY HANDSOME!

—SIR CHULLY-BOY BAXTER
SAN ANTONIO, TX

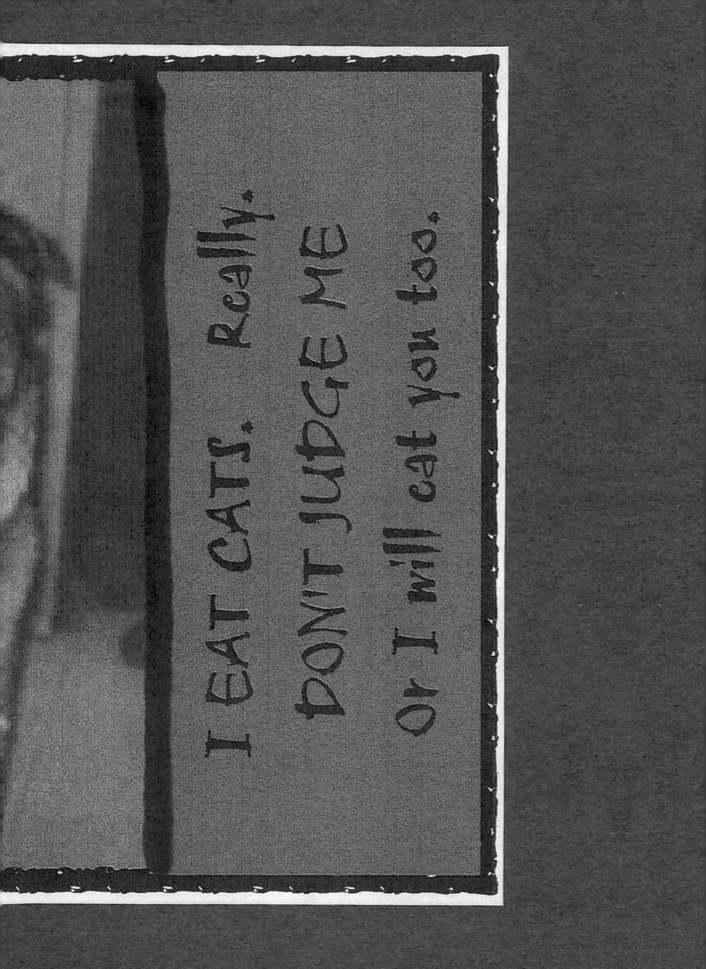

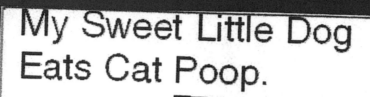

My Sweet Little Dog
Eats Cat Poop.

And then tries
to give me a kiss.

THERE'S NOTHING
LIKE A WET NOSE
PRESSING INTO
THE BACKS OF YOUR
KNEES EVERY MORNING
TO MAKE YOU RUSH
TO THE FOOD BOWL!

Dogfession:

I just turned down a vacation
because I didn't want to be without
the dogs for 2 weeks

I know he's not a kid,
but . . .

I never had one.

I know what "NO" means.
I just like to Bark.

I sometimes think
the carpet is grass

Don't come any closer, I will JUMP!!

WHICH DO I LOVE MORE?
HUSBAND?
DOGS?
BEACH?

FOR THE SAKE OF MY MARRIAGE
I CAN'T TELL YOU.

Dogfession: I don't like kids in _MY car.

Getting into the fridge is MUCH
harder than it looks on TV!

I know it is raining out
and as long as I am STILL TECHNICALLY
in my bed,

they won't make me go outside.

The window of your soul can be seen by your dog.

I'm NOT "second hand."
I'm NOT "recycled."
I'm not a "pound puppy."
Someone just wanted me twice!

I've been gone 10 years and my mom still misses me.

1962 Spooky 1977

Somebody dropped him off
to be euthanized.
He was just 6 months old.
We've had him for
10 years now.

They don't know he is alive.
...I hope they still feel guilty.

I miss Bobby Blue
more than anybody I knew that died

I've danced so much . . . . Things are looking blurry!

I HATE WINTER

Life is so much easier as a dog!!!

At least once a month, I tell my dog how lucky she is that she does not have to pluck chin whiskers or bleach mustache hairs!

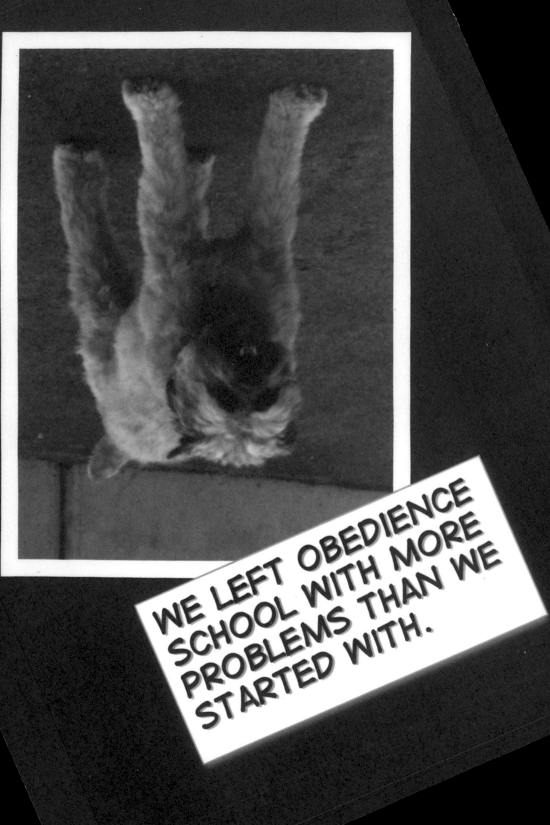

WE LEFT OBEDIENCE SCHOOL WITH MORE PROBLEMS THAN WE STARTED WITH.

My voice gets two octaves higher

whenever I see this face.

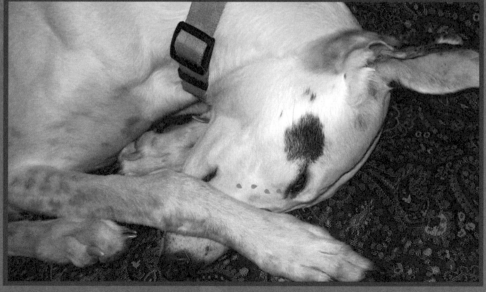

I CRY A LOT WHEN MY OWNERS LEAVE...

but you would never guess I do.

i don't hear
so i never have
to listen.
goo-goo
gah-gah
goo-goo-gah
gah-gah-goo!
BUS

My
Dogfession:
I'm cute, I'm
just NOT
photogenic!

**My dog will do anything for me...
if she feels like it.**

when i was a kid
i used to bring stray dogs
home and hide them
in my room and when
i'd get caught
i'd pretend that
they were the family
dog and had been
there all along.

it never worked.

I hate when they talk about how old he is getting in front of him.. If we don't tell him He'll never know!

...I wish he had 13 more years.

Sometimes, I see them at the window... still...

KoKo 1988-2003   Baxter 1992-2006

Chili

When I get to the Rainbow Bridge
I hope Chili is there.

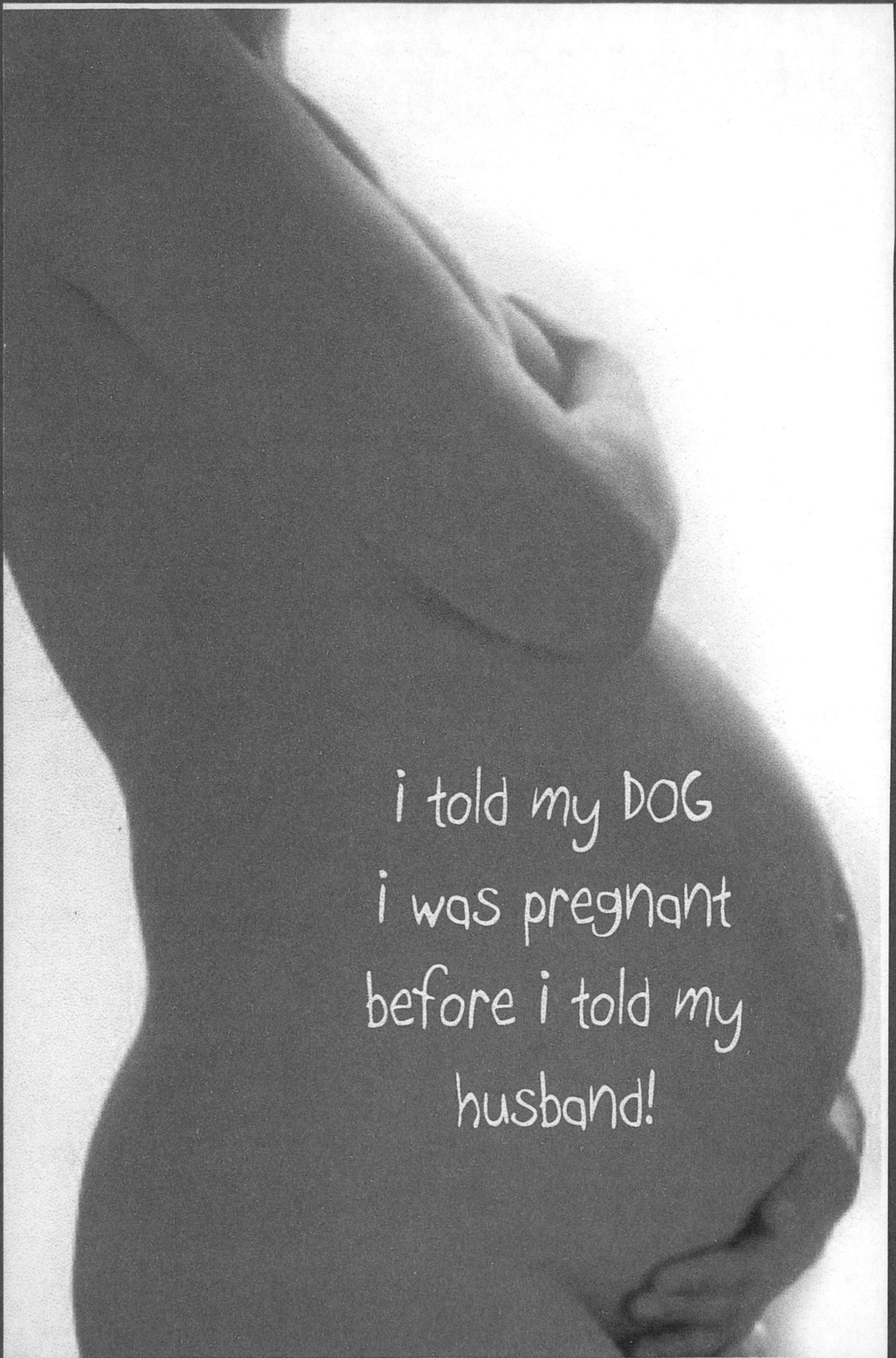

i told my DOG
i was pregnant
before i told my
husband!

she is the only child I will ever have

I want to change bodies with my doggie so I can talk to her.

Brandon-4 years old

when people show me pictures of their kids, i show them pictures of my dog

CURSES TO HE
WHO MESSES
WITH MY ELMO.

THIS DOG ALWAYS TRIES TO BITE ME. NOW IT'S MY TURN!!!!!!!!!!!

I AM NOT MEAN Just in Love

My dogfession:
I lie about my age. Hey--
it's rude to ask a lady how
old she is. Mama now fibs
for me and sometimes I can
even pass for a puppy!

Dogfession to my Mom

I farted.
You blamed Daddy.
It wasn't him... This time.

It's not easy running a casino or being in the racketeering business. Everyday, my mother leaves for work (God bless her soul) and the coffee table becomes a blackjack table. Everyday, I worry about the undercover agents on my tail.

It's no secret that being in this business is ruff. As a pitbull/chocolate lab mix, I'm the Sonny to my predecessor, Cinque's, Michael Corleone. Man, that chocolate lab was smooth.

Everyday, I also worry that my temperament will get the best of me. A cool, calm head is important in this business. It's essential, really, to stay alive.

I pretend to enjoy this.
So I don't hurt Mommy's feelings.

I pretend like the dogs wear their doggles when the car window is open for their protection, it's really 'cause I like seeing what other motorists do when they see my dogs looking so silly.

My Spidey Sense Says
That Somethings
Not Quite Right Here.

THIS IS OUR DOG - CHAMPAGNE - IN HER HALLOWEEN COSTUME. HER DOGFESSION IS THAT SHE LIKES TO WEAR THE COSTUME EVEN WHEN IT'S NOT HALLOWEEN!

Trick or Treat?

Somone I know got the treats (He stole a LOT of halloween candy & ate it all)

I got the trick had to pay a vet bill AND Clean the carpets!

BOO!

Another Day at the Office...

I am about to do something you're not going to like...

but know I feel bad about it.

**FAIRY PRINCESS WHO
CAME TO EARTH IN CUTEST COSTUME
AVAILABLE THAT DAY**

I SHARE EVERYTHING WITH MY BEST FRIEND.

Don't utter this to anyone, but my girlfriend's a cow.

Yes, You MAY adore me.

SERVE ME!

The Police were right...what was that guy thinking when he broke in the back door? Did he think I was all alone?

I am forever grateful to Molly for saving my life.

I took Fitzgerald to one of those "Blessing of the Beast" events but we left in the middle. It seemed redundant. Dogs, by nature, are a blessing.

This is why
we don't have
ANY nice furniture.

I don't like strangers touching my head. And no, I wasn't abused, I just don't like it.   MOJO

He told me we *lived* in *England*, not *Narnia*. *I was only* *sniffing* at the back of his wardrobe!

I feed the strays
that come into the yard at our business
when no one is looking
and then pretend I don't know
why they won't leave.

THE FIRST THING I LEARNED TO DRAW, IN KINDERGARTEN WHEN I WAS FIVE... WAS A DOG!

30 YEARS LATER...

I'M STILL FIGURING OUT HOW TO DRAW A DOG...

Don't they make me look smart?

Before I was adopted, I was homeless, had 7 boyfriends and was an unwed mother.
- Ebony

my $20.00 shelter dog has cost me over $15,000.00

can't buy me ♥ LoVe ♥

Deck Boards - $90.00

Rabbit - $20.00

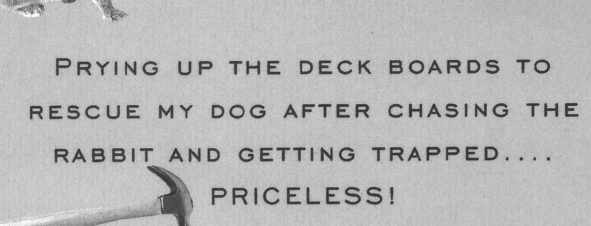

Prying up the deck boards to rescue my dog after chasing the rabbit and getting trapped.... PRICELESS!

I wish I never neutered my dog.

Now I'm going to have to clone him

and that's going to cost a lot more than puppies!

At times,
I do think

"NOSE
JOB...."

When I grow up, I want to be just like my BIG sister!

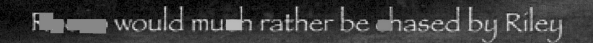

would much rather be chased by Riley

than stroked by me

Ok. I'll move over.

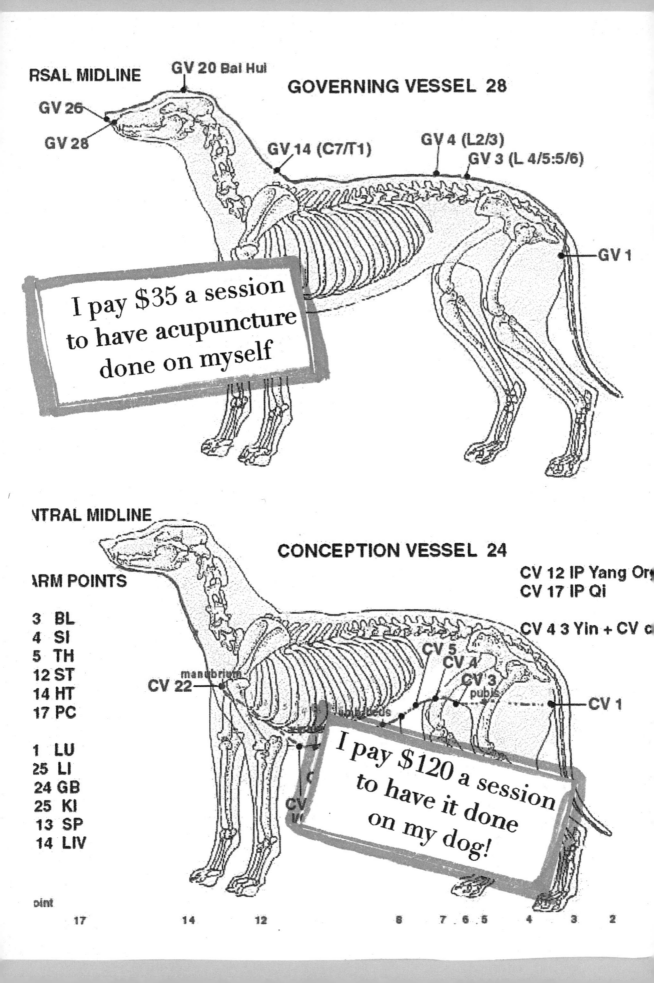

I dogsat Elvis for a week.

He snores. loud. I miss it.

There is **NOTHING** anyone can say to convince me that my dog isn't going to live forever.

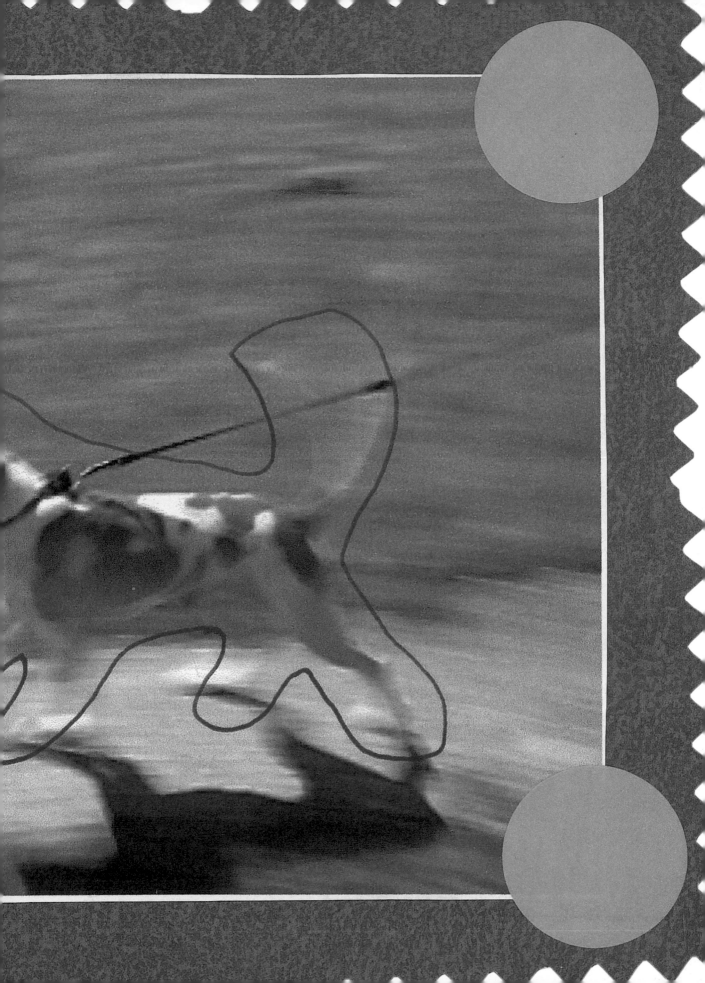

IS IT WRONG TO BE THIS HANDSOME?

THEN I DON'T WANT TO BE RIGHT.

While on Vacation without the dogs, I call them on the phone. Usually they don't respond, but I can hear them breathing.

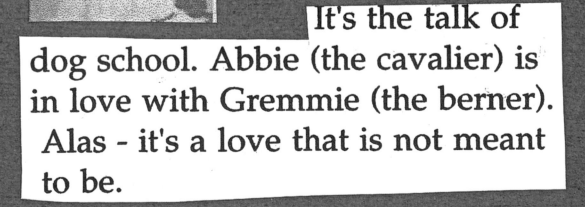

It's the talk of dog school. Abbie (the cavalier) is in love with Gremmie (the berner). Alas - it's a love that is not meant to be.

Dear Dylan **loved** biscuits and Hedgie, but what he loved **most** of all was **my mom**

I
ask
my grandma to
pray for the dogs that
need homes even though
I'm not one who goes to church.

My Friend wrote this poem for her missing dog 2 years ago. It still makes me cry.

A Prayer for Drew

Everyday I pray-

Everyday I pray
    that today will be the day Drew comes home
everyday I pray
    that Drew is being well cared for
everyday I pray
    that this will all be over soon

Everyday I pray
    that whoever has Drew knows how much he is loved
everyday I pray
    that whoever has Drew knows how many people are affected
everyday I pray
    that whoever has Drew has a conscience

Everyday I pray
    that I will walk outside and find Drew on the front porch
everyday I pray
    that as I drive past the park I will see Drew standing in the middle of it
everyday I pray
    that I will get a phone call to go pick up Drew

Everyday I pray
    that today my baby boy is home safe and sound

Will You Pray With Me?

DOGFESSION:

My dogs will be VERY UPSET if they are not included in the DOGFESSION book! I am thinking I should start saving up for their doggie mental therapy, just in case.

My cheeks hurt

mom...

take the picture already!

She makes me look for the bright side of things.

Mom, please don't tell Dad the cat and I
have strategy sessions when we're not home.

This is
ot my
dog...

I saved her as my wallpaper. I get more compliments on my baby than a co-worker who just returned from maternity leave!

An open box of biscuits....
just sitting there!

He wonders... What would SCOOBY doo?

This puppy was a DEMON in a previous life

you want a piece of me ?)

Every time Libby lunges
at a bicycle, wheelchair, or stroller,
I pretend that it's the first time
that has ever happened.

No BUTTs about it.

Beau has the cutest heiny in town.

He's got the Terrible Twos - and he's just turned One.

It's hard to stick to the training when you have these eyes looking at you.

My dog has two little swirls on his butt that I think are so cute. I circle my finger over each one and say "butt swirls" as he tucks his fanny under!

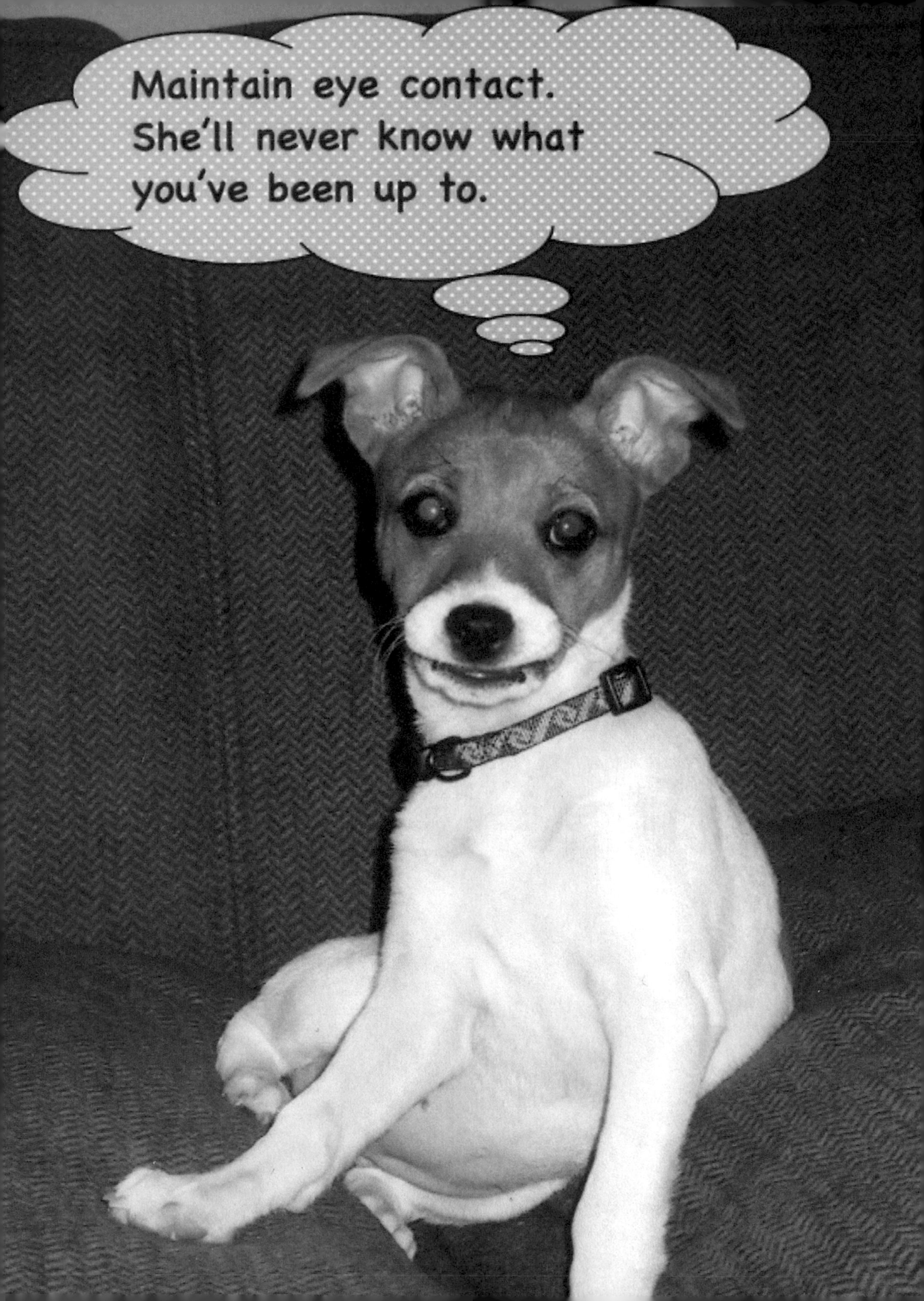
Maintain eye contact.
She'll never know what
you've been up to.

I wish
I could
Say they
look at me
like this
out
of love
for me..

but its
really
the love
of
cookies
that
gets
this
look.

Yes - An entire pound of turkey hot dogs CAN fit into a 12 lb. dog.

However
it is not at all recommended if you have new carpeting like I did.

My dog LOVES dirty laundry!!!

Kylie's Dogfession: I like to have a tail & be a dog.

Note:
Kylie is 3 years old. We stuff the dog's stuffed snakes down the back of her pants and she is a "dog" all night long doing Sit! Down! & Stay! - she drew this herself.

MY NAME IS CHANEL

AND I'M A SOCK-A-HOLIC!!!!!

HE THINKS
IF HE CONCENTRATES
HARD ENOUGH, A TREAT WILL F
FROM HEAVEN JUST FOR HIM.

SOMETIMES HE'S RIGHT.

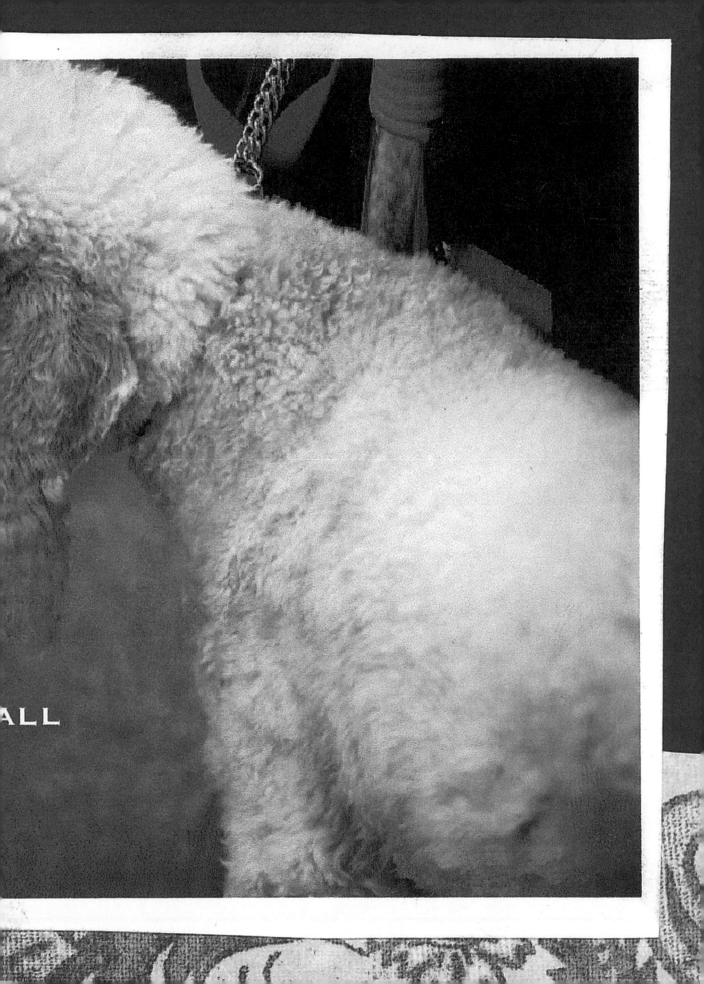

We are lawbreakers.

We let them play off leash when no one is around.

I Trained my Gramma to bake me FRESH SALMON !!!

(I told her my mommy never feeds me)

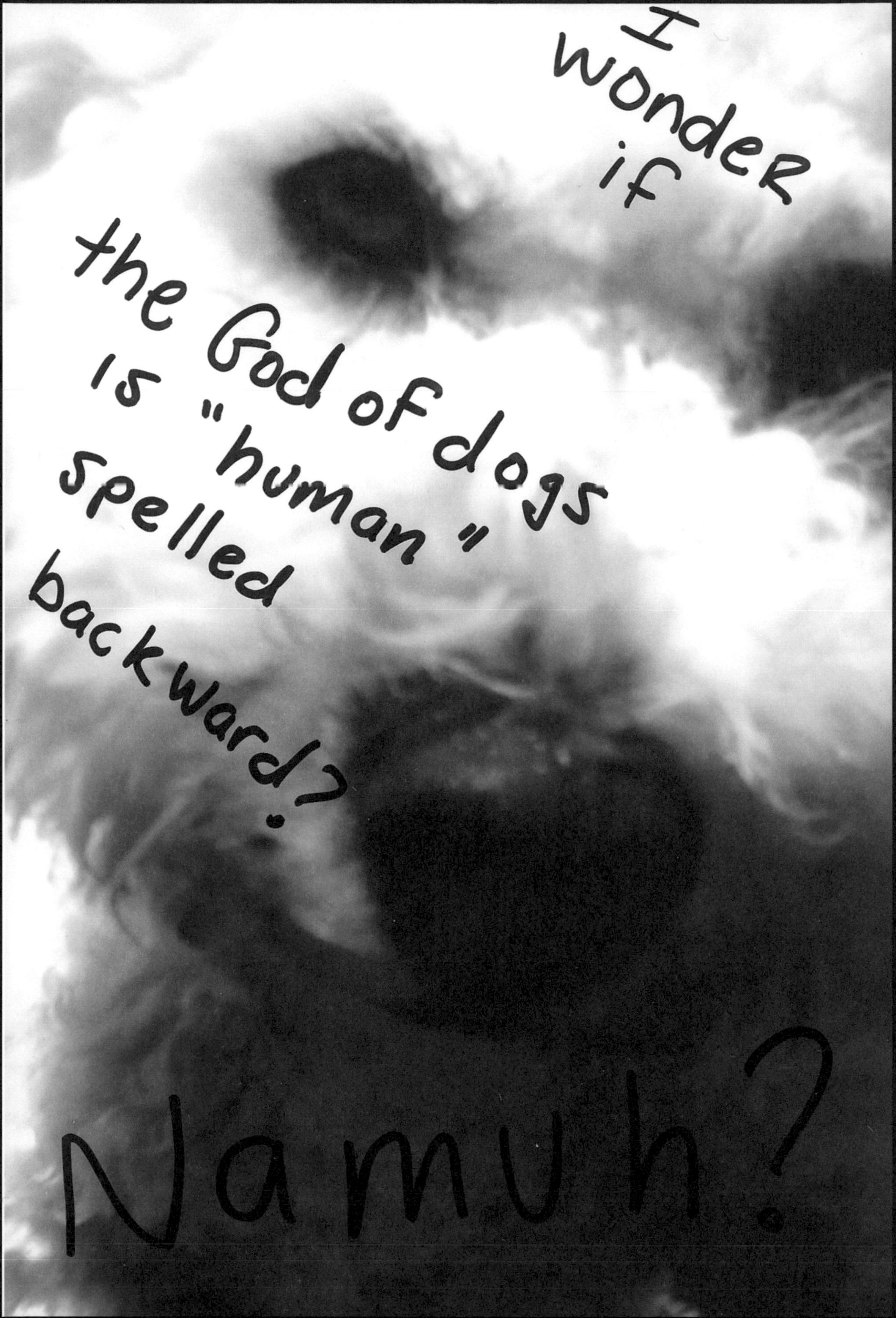
I wonder if
the God of dogs
is "human"
spelled
backward?
Namuh?

AN ARMY OF TWO

Will play for treats and belly rubs!

Separated At Birth

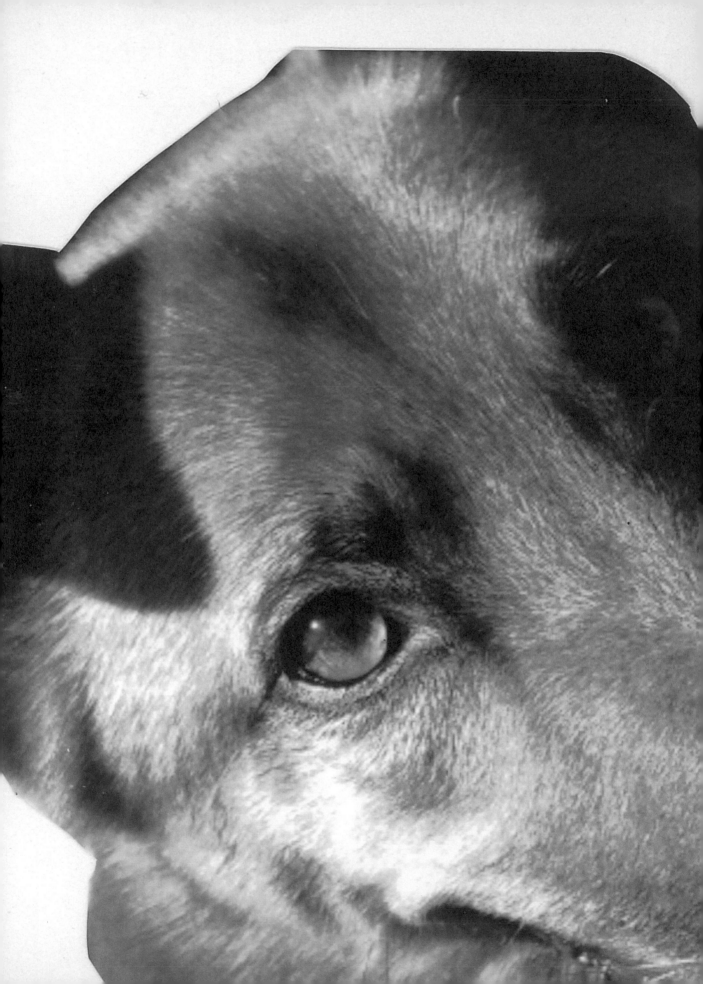

"I will not go outside on my walk if...

winds exceed 30mph

it's earlier than 5am

colder than 30 degrees

or... looks like rain SORRY!

I will not eat my bowl of dog food unless it's sprinkled with Parmesan cheese!

Thank God I have a dog or else
i'd just be talking to myself.

Dogfession

Late at night, I whisper to my dog...If you were a man, I'd marry you".

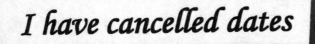

I have cancelled dates

to stay home and watch my puppy sleep.

I came around a corner and caught my boyfriend HITTING my dog.... then HE HIT THE Road!

Dear Dogfessions,

My mama was dating a  that I didn't like, so I chewed the antenna off of his

My mama defended me, and the dumped her.

Now my mama drives the speed limit everywhere she goes.

P.S.—Do I really look like a criminal?

Sometimes Lacey-Jane wants her new brother Bogey to GO AWAY

OUTSIDE

INSIDE

She doesn't realize that a 14 year old
Maltese doesn't really scare anyone.
Please Humor Her.

I slept on your
new cashmere
sweater while you
were at work

Sometimes I like to pretend

that I am Toto

and my mom is

the Wicked Witch of the West